SEEDTIME AND HARVEST

Neville Goddard

CLASSY
PUBLISHING

SEEDTIME AND HARVEST
by Neville Goddard

Published by Classy Publishing, 2023

www.classypublishing.com
info@classypublishing.com

ISBN: 978-93-5522-315-9

Typeset in Minion Pro
Cover Design by Classy Publishing

CONTENTS

CHAPTER 1

The End of the Golden String

I Give you the end of a golden string;
Only wind it into a ball,
It will lead you in at Heaven's gate,
Built in Jerusalem's wall.

—William Blake

In the following essays I have tried to indicate certain ways of approach to the understanding of the Bible and the realization of your dreams.

That ye be not slothful, but followers of them who through faith and patience inherit the promises.

—Hebrews 6:12

Many who enjoy the old familiar verses of Scripture are discouraged when they themselves try to read the Bible as they would any other book because, quite excusably, they do not understand that the Bible is written in the language of symbolism. Not knowing that all of its characters are personifications of the laws and functions of mind; that the Bible is psychology rather than history, they puzzle their brains over it for a while and then give up. It is all too mystifying. To understand the significance of its imagery, the reader of the Bible must be imaginatively awake.

According to the Scriptures, we sleep with Adam and wake with Christ. That is, we sleep collectively and wake individually.

> *And the Lord God caused a deep sleep to fall upon Adam, and he slept.*
>
> —Genesis 2:21

If Adam, or generic man, is in a deep sleep, then his experiences as recorded in the Scriptures must be a dream. Only he who is awake can tell his dream, and only he would understand the symbolism of dreams can interpret the dream.

> *And they said one to another, "Did not our heart burn within us, while he talked with us by the way, and while he opened to us the Scriptures?"*
>
> —Luke 24:32

The Bible is a revelation of the laws and functions of Mind expressed in the language of that twilight realm into which we go when we sleep. Because the symbolical language of this twilight realm is much the same for all men, the recent explorers of this realm (human imagination) call it the "collective unconscious."

The purpose of this book, however, is not to give you a complete definition of Biblical symbols or exhaustive interpretations of its stories.

All I hope to have done is to have indicated the way in which you are most likely to succeed in realizing your desires.

"What things soever ye desire" can be obtained only through the conscious, voluntary exercise of imagination in direct obedience to the laws of Mind.

Somewhere within this realm of imagination there is a mood, a feeling of the wish fulfilled which, if appropriated, means success to you.

This realm, this Eden — your imagination — is vaster than you know and repays exploration.

"I give you the end of a golden string." You must wind it into a ball.

CHAPTER 2

The Four Mighty Ones

And a river went out of Eden to water the garden; and from thence it was parted, and became into four heads."

—Genesis 2:10

"And every one had four faces:

—Ezekiel 10:14

"I see four men loose, walking in the midst of the fire, and they have no hurt; and the form of the fourth is like the Son of God.

—Daniel 3:25

"Four Mighty Ones are in every man.

—William Blake

The "Four Mighty Ones" constitute the selfhood of man, or God in man. There are "Four Mighty Ones" in every man, but these "Four Mighty Ones" are not four separate beings, separated one from the other as are the fingers of his hand.

The "Four Mighty Ones" are four different aspects of his mind, and differ from one another in function and character without being four separate selves inhabiting one man's body.

The "Four Mighty Ones" may be equated with the four Hebrew characters: [Yodh, He, Waw, He, from right to left] which form the four-lettered mystery name of the Creative Power ["Yahweh" or even occasionally as "Jehovah"] from and combining within itself the past, present and future forms of the verb "to be."

The Tetragrammaton is revered as the symbol of the Creative Power in man: I AM. The creative four functions in man reaching forth to realize in actual material phenomena qualities latent in Itself.

We can best understand the "Four Mighty Ones" by comparing them to the four most important characters in the production of a play.

All the world's a stage,
And all the men and women merely players;
They have their exits and their entrances;
And one man in his time plays many parts . . .
—As You Like It, Act II, Scene VII

The producer, the author, the director and the actor are the four most important characters in the production of a play.

In the drama of life, the producer's function is to suggest the theme of a play. This he does in the form of a wish, such as, "I wish I were successful"; "I wish I could take a trip"; "I wish I were married, and so on. But to appear on the world's stage, these general themes must somehow be specified and worked out in detail. It is not enough to say, "I wish I were successful" - that is too vague. Successful at what?

However, the first "Mighty One" only suggests a theme.

The dramatization of the theme is left to the originality of the second "Might One", the author.

In dramatizing the theme, the author writes only the last scene of the play - but this scene he writes in detail.

The scene must dramatize the wish fulfilled. He mentally constructs as life-like a scene as possible of what he would experience had he realized his wish. When the scene is clearly visualized, the author's work is done.

The third "Mighty One" in the production of life's play is the director. The director's tasks are to see that the actor remains faithful to the script and to rehearse him over and over again until he is natural in the part.

This function may be likened to a controlled and consciously directed attention; an attention focused exclusively on the action which implies that the wish is already realized.

"The form of the Fourth is like the Son of God" - human imagination, the actor.

This fourth "Mighty One" performs within himself, in imagination, the pre-determined action which implies the fulfillment of the wish. This function does not visualize or observe the action. This function actually enacts the drama, and does it over and over again until it takes on the tones of reality.

Without the dramatized vision of fulfilled desire, the theme remains a mere theme and sleeps forever in the vast chambers of unborn themes. Nor without the co-operant attention, obedient to the dramatized vision of fulfilled desire, will the vision perceived attain objective reality.

The "Four Mighty Ones" are the four quarters of the human soul. The first is Jehovah's King, who suggests the theme; the second is Jehovah's servant, who faithfully works out the theme in a dramatic vision; the third is Jehovah's man, who was attentive and obedient to the vision of fulfilled desire, who brings the wandering imagination back to the script "seventy times seven". The "Form of the Fourth" is Jehovah himself, who enacts the dramatized theme on the stage of the mind.

Let this mind be in you, which was also in Christ Jesus: Who, being in the form of God, thought it not robbery to be equal with God. . .

—Philippians 2:5,6

The drama of life is a joint effort of the four quarters of the human soul.

All that you behold, though' it appears without, it is within, in your imagination, of which this world of mortality is but a shadow.

—Blake

All that we behold is a visual construction contrived to express a theme - a theme which has been dramatized, rehearsed and performed elsewhere. What we are witnessing on the stage of the world is an optical construction devised to express the themes which have been dramatized, rehearsed and performed in the imagination of men.

The "Four Mighty Ones" constitute the Selfhood of man, or God in man: and all that man beholds, though' it appears without, are but shadows cast upon the screen of space - optical constructions contrived by Selfhood to inform him in regard to the themes which he has conceived, dramatized, rehearsed and performed within himself.

"The creature was made subject unto vanity" that he may become conscious of Selfhood and its functions, for with consciousness of Selfhood and its functions, he can act to a purpose; he can have a consciously self-determined history.

Without consciousness, he acts unconsciously, and cries to an objective God to save him from his own creation.

> *O Lord, how long shall I cry, and*
> *Thou wilt not hear! Even cry out*
> *unto Thee of violence, and*
> *Thou wilt not save!*
>
> —Habakkuk 1:2

When man discovers that life is a play which he, himself, is consciously or unconsciously writing, he will cease from the blind, self-torture of executing judgment upon others.

Instead, he will rewrite the play to conform to his ideal, for he will realize that all changes in the play must come from the cooperation of the "Four Mighty Ones" within himself. They alone can alter the script and produce the change.

All the men and women in his world are merely players and are as helpless to change his play as are the players on the screen of the theatre to change the picture. The desired change must be conceived, dramatized, rehearsed and performed in the theatre of his mind.

When the fourth function, the imagination, has completed its task of rehearsing the revised version of the play until it is natural, then the curtain will rise upon this so seemingly solid world and the "Mighty Four" will cast a shadow of the real play upon the screen of space.

Men and women will automatically play their parts to bring about the fulfillment of the dramatized theme. The players, by reason of their various parts in the world's drama, become relevant to the individual's dramatized theme and, because relevant, are drawn into his drama. They will play their parts, faithfully believing all the while that it was they themselves who initiated the parts they play. This they do because:

> *Thou, Father, art in me, and I in thee,*
> *. . . I in them, and thou in me.*
>
> —John 17:21, 23

I am involved in mankind. We are one. We are all playing the four parts of producer, author, director and actor in the drama of life. Some of us are doing it consciously, others unconsciously. It is necessary that we do it consciously. Only in this way can we be certain of a perfect ending to our play. Then we shall understand why we must become conscious of the four functions of the one God within ourselves that we may have the companionship of God as His Sons.

Man should not stay a man:
His aim should higher be.
For God will only gods
Accept as company.

—Angelus Silesius

In January of 1946, I took my wife and little daughter to Barbados in the British West Indies for a holiday. Not knowing there were any difficulties in getting a return passage, I had not booked ours before leaving New York. Upon our arrival in Barbados I discovered that there were only two ships serving the islands, one from Boston and one from New York. I was told there was no available space on either ship before September. As I had commitments in New York for the first week in May, I put my name on the long waiting list for the April sailing.

A few days later, the ship from New York was anchored in the harbor. I observed it very carefully, and decided that this was the ship we should take. I returned to my hotel and determined on an inner action that would be mine were we actually sailing on that ship. I settled down in an easy chair in my bedroom, to lose myself in this imaginative action.

In Barbados, we take a motor launch or rowboat out into the deep harbor when we embark on a large steamer. I knew I must catch the feeling that we were sailing on that ship. I chose the inner action of stepping from the tender and climbing up the gangplank of the steamer. The first time I tried, my attention wandered after I had reached the top of the gangplank. I brought myself back down, and tried again and again. I do not recall how many times I carried out this action in my imagination until I reached the deck and looked back at the port with the feeling of sweet sadness at departing. I was happy to be returning to my home in New York, but nostalgic in saying goodbye to the lovely island and our family and friends. I do recall that in one of my many attempts at walking up the gangplank in the feeling that I was sailing, I fell asleep. After I awoke, I went about the usual social activities of the day and evening.

The following morning, I received a call from the steamship company requesting me to come down to their office and pick up our tickets for the April sailing. I was curious to know why Barbados had been chosen to receive the cancellation and why I, at the end of the long waiting list, was to have the reservation, but all that the agent could tell me was that a cable had been received that morning from New York, offering passage for three. I was not the first the agent had called, but for reasons she could not explain, those she had called said that now they found it inconvenient to sail in April. We sailed on April 20th and arrived in New York on the morning of May the first.

In the production of my play - the sailing on a boat that would bring me to New York by the first of May - I played the four most important characters in my drama. As the producer, I decided to sail on a specific ship at a certain time. Playing the part of the author, I wrote the script - I visualized the inner action which conformed to the outer action I would take if my desire were realized. As the director, I rehearsed myself, the actor, in that imagined action of climbing the gangplank until that action felt completely natural.

This being done, events and people moved swiftly to conform, in the outer world, to the play I had constructed and enacted in my imagination.

I saw the mystic vision flow
And live in men and woods and streams.
Until I could no longer know
The stream of life from my own dreams.
—George William Russell (AE)

I told this story to an audience of mine in San Francisco, and a lady in the audience told me how she had unconsciously used the same technique when she was a young girl.

The incident occurred on Christmas Eve. She was feeling very sad and tired and sorry for herself. Her father, whom she adored, had died suddenly. Not only did she feel this loss at the Christmas season, but necessity had forced her to give up her planned college years and go to work. This rainy Christmas Eve she was riding home on a San Diego street car. The car was filled with gay chatter of happy young people home for the holidays. To hide her tears from those rounds about her, she stood on the open part at the front of the car and turned her face into the skies to mingle her tears with the rain. With her eyes closed, and holding the rail of the car firmly, this is what she said to herself: "This is not the salt of the tears that I taste, but the salt of the sea in the wind. This is not San Diego, this is the South Pacific and I am sailing into the Bay of Samoa". And looking up, in her imagination, she constructed what she imagined to be the Southern Cross. She lost herself in this contemplation so that all faded round about her. Suddenly she was at the end of the line, and home.

Two weeks later, she received word from a lawyer in Chicago that he was holding three thousand dollars in American bonds for her. Several years before, an aunt of hers had gone to Europe, with instructions that these bonds be turned over to her niece if she did not return to the United States. The lawyer had just received word of the aunt's death, and was now carrying out her instructions.

A month later, this girl sailed for the islands in the South Pacific. It was night when she entered the Bay of Samoa. Looking down, she could see the white foam like a "bone in the lady's mouth" as the ship ploughed through the waves, and brought the salt of the sea in the wind. An officer on duty said to her: "There is the Southern Cross", and looking up, she saw the Southern Cross as she had imagined it.

In the intervening years, she had many opportunities to use her imagination constructively, but as she had done this unconsciously, she did not realize there was a Law behind it all. Now that she understands, she, too, is consciously playing her four major roles in the daily drama of her life, producing plays for the good of others as well as herself.

> *Then the soldiers, when they had crucified Jesus, took his garments, and made four parts, to every soldier a part; and also his coat; now the coat was without seam, woven from the top throughout."*
>
> —John 19:23

CHAPTER 3

The Gift of Faith

And the Lord had respect unto Abel and in his offerings; But unto Cain and to his offering he had no respect.

—Genesis 4:4, 5

If we search the Scriptures, we will become aware of a far deeper meaning in the above quotation than that which a literal reading would give us. The Lord is no other than your own consciousness:

. . . say unto the children of Israel, I AM hath sent me unto you.

—Exodus 3:14.

"I AM" is the self-definition of the Lord.

Cain and Abel, as the grandchildren of the Lord, can be only personifications of two distinct functions of your own consciousness. The author is really concerned to show the "Two Contrary States of the Human Soul," and he has used two brothers to show these states. The two brothers represent two distinct outlooks on the world possessed by everyone. One is the limited perception of the senses, and the other is an imaginative view of the world. Cain - the first view - is a passive surrender to appearances and an acceptance of life on the basis of the world without: a view which inevitably leads to unsatisfied longing or a contentment with disillusion. Abel - the second view - is a vision of fulfilled desire, lifting man above the evidence of the senses to that state of relief where he no longer pines with desire. Ignorance of the second view is a soul on fire. Knowledge of the second view is the wing whereby it flies to the Heaven of fulfilled desire.

> *Come, eat my bread and drink of the wind that*
> *I have mingled, forsake the foolish and live.*
> —Proverbs 9:56

In the epistle to the Hebrews, the writer tells us that Abel's offering was faith, and, states the author:

> *Without faith it is impossible to please Him.*
> —Hebrews 11:6

> *"Now faith is the substance of things hoped for,*
> *the evidence of things not seen. . . Through faith*

we understand that the worlds were framed by the word of God, so that things which are seen were not made of things which do appear.

—Hebrews 11:1, 3

Cain offers the evidence of the senses which consciousness, the Lord, rejects, because acceptance of this gift as a mold of the future would mean the fixation and perpetuation of the present state forever. The sick would be sick, the poor would be poor, the thief would be a thief, the murderer a murderer, and so on, without hope of redemption.

The Lord, or consciousness, has no respect for such passive use of imagination - which is the gift of Cain. He delights in the gift of Abel, the active, voluntary, loving exercise of the imagination on behalf of man for himself and others.

Let the weak man say, I am strong.

—Joel 3:10

Let man disregard appearances and declare himself to be the man he wants to be. Let him imagine beauty where his senses reveal ashes, joy where they testify to mourning, riches where they bear witness to poverty. Only by such active, voluntary use of imagination can man be lifted up and Eden restored.

The ideal is always waiting to be incarnated, but unless we ourselves offer the ideal to the Lord, our consciousness, by assuming that we are already that which we seek to embody, it is incapable of birth. The Lord needs his daily lamb of faith to mold the world in harmony with our dreams.

> *By faith Abel offered unto God a more excellent sacrifice than Cain.*
>
> —Hebrews 11:4

Faith sacrifices the apparent fact for the unapparent truth. Faith holds fast to the fundamental truth that through the medium of an assumption, invisible states become visible facts.

> *For what is faith unless it is to believe what you do not see?*
>
> —St. Augustine

Just recently, I had the opportunity to observe the wonderful results of one who had the faith to believe what she did not see.

A young woman asked me to meet her sister and her three-year-old nephew. He was a fine, healthy lad with clear blue eyes and an exceptionally fine unblemished skin. Then, she told me her story.

At birth, the boy was perfect in every way save for a large, ugly birthmark covering one side of his face. Their doctor advised them that nothing could be done for this type of scar. Visits to many specialists only confirmed his statement. Hearing the verdict, the aunt set herself the task of proving her faith - that an assumption, though denied by the evidence of the senses, if persisted in, will harden into fact.

Every time she thought of the baby, which was often, she saw, in her imagination, an eight month-old baby with a perfect face - without any trace of a scar. This was not easy, but she knew that in this case, that was the gift of Abel which pleased God. She persisted in her faith - she believed what was not there to be seen. The result was that she visited her sister on the child's eight-month birthday and found him to have a perfect, unblemished skin with no trace of a birthmark ever having been present. "Luck! Coincidence! Shouts Cain. No. Abel knows that these are names given by those who have no faith, to the works of faith.

We walk by faith, not by sight.

—2 Corinthians 5:7

When reason and the facts of life oppose the idea you desire to realize and you accept the evidence of your senses and the dictates of reason as the truth, you have brought the Lord – your consciousness - the gift of Cain. It is obvious that such offerings do not please Him.

Life on earth is a training ground for image making. If you use only the molds which your senses dictate, there will be no change in your life. You are here to live the more abundant life, so you must use the invisible molds of imagination and make results and accomplishments the crucial test of your power to create. Only as you assume the feeling of the wish fulfilled and continue therein are you offering the gift that pleases.

When Abel's gift is my attire,
Then I'll realize my desire.

The Prophet Malachi complains that man has robbed God:

> *But ye say, Wherein have we robbed thee? In tithes and offerings.*
>
> —Malachi 3:8

Facts based upon reason and the evidence of the senses which oppose the idea seeking expression, rob you of the belief in the reality of the invisible state. But "faith is the evidence of things not seen," and through it "Good calleth those things which be not as though they were" [Romans 4:17].

Call the thing not seen; assume the feeling of your wish fulfilled.

> *. . .that there may be meat in mine house, and prove me now herewith, sayeth the Lord of hosts, if I will not open you the windows of heaven, and pour you out a blessing, that there shall not be room enough to receive it.*
>
> —Malachi 3:10

This is the story of a couple living in Sacramento, California, who refused to accept the evidence of their senses, who refused to be robbed in spite of a seeming loss. The wife had given her husband a very valuable wristwatch. The gift doubled its value because of the sentiment he attached to it. They had a little ritual with the watch. Every night as he removed the watch he gave it to her and she put it away in a special box in the bureau. Every morning she took the watch and gave it to him to put on.

One morning the watch was missing. They both remembered playing their usual parts the night before, therefore the watch was not lost or misplaced, but stolen. Then and there, they determined not to accept the fact that it was really gone. They said to each other, "This is an opportunity to practice what we believe." They decided that, in their imagination, they would enact their customary ritual as though the watch were actually there. In his imagination, every night the husband took off the watch and gave it to his wife, while in her imagination she accepted the watch and carefully put it away. Every morning she removed the watch from its box and gave it to her husband and he, in turn, put it on. This they did faithfully for two weeks.

After their fourteen-day vigil, a man went into the one and only jewellery store in Sacramento where the watch would be recognized. As he offered a gem for appraisal, the owner of the store noticed the wristwatch he was wearing. Under the pretext of needing a closer examination of the stone, he went into an inner office and called the police. After the police arrested the man, they found in his apartment over ten thousand dollars worth of stolen jewellery. In walking "by faith, not by sight", this couple attained their desire - the watch - and also aided many others in regaining what had seemed to be lost forever.

> *If one advances confidently in the direction of his dream, and endeavors to live the life which he has imagined, he will meet with a success unexpected in common hours.*
>
> —Thoreau

CHAPTER 4

The Scale of Being

And he dreamed, and behold a ladder set up on the earth, and the top of it reached to heaven: and behold the angels of God ascending and descending on it. And, behold, the Lord stood above it. . .

—Genesis 28:12, 13

In a dream, in a vision of the night, when deep sleep fell upon Jacob, his inner eye was opened and he beheld the world as a series of ascending and descending levels of awareness. It was a revelation of the deepest insight into the mysteries of the world. Jacob saw a vertical scale of ascending and descending values, or states of consciousness. This gave meaning to everything in the outer world, for without such a scale of values there would be no meaning to life.

At every moment of time, man stands upon the eternal scale of meaning. There is no object or event that has ever taken place or is taking place now that is without significance. The significance of an object or event for the individual is a direct index to the level of his consciousness.

You are holding this book, for example. On one level of consciousness, it is an object in space.

On a higher level, it is a series of letters on paper, arranged according to certain rules. On a still higher level, it is an expression of meaning.

Looking outwardly, you see the book first, but actually, the meaning comes first. It occupies a higher grade of significance than the letter arrangement on paper or the book as an object in space. Meaning determined the arrangement of letters; the arrangement of letters only expresses the meaning. The meaning is invisible and above the level of the visible arrangement of letters. If there had been no meaning to be expressed, no book would have been written and published.

And, behold, the Lord stood above it.

The Lord and meaning are one - the Creator, the cause of the phenomena of life.

In the beginning was the Word, and the Word was with God, and the Word was God.

—John 1:1

In the beginning was the intention - the meaning - and the intention was with the intender, and the intention was the intender. The objects and events in time and space occupy a lower level of significance than the level of meaning which produced them. All things were made by meaning, and without meaning was not anything made that was made. The fact that everything seen can be regarded as the effect, on a lower level of significance, of an unseen higher order of significance is a very important one to grasp.

Our usual mode of procedure is to attempt to explain the higher levels of significance - why things happen - in terms of the lower - what and how things happen. For example, let us take an actual accident and try to explain it.

Most of us live on the level of what happened - the accident was an event in space - one automobile struck another and practically demolished it. Some of us live on the higher level of "how" the accident happened - it was a rainy night, the roads were slippery and the second car skidded into the first. On rare occasions, a few of us reach the highest or causal level of "why" such an accident occurs. Then we become aware of the invisible, the state of consciousness which produced the visible event.

In this case, the ruined car was driven by a widow, who, though she felt she could not afford to, greatly desired to change her environment. Having heard that, by the proper use of her imagination, she could do and be all she wished to be, this widow had been imagining herself actually living in the city of her desire. At the same time, she was living in a consciousness of loss, both personal and financial. Therefore, she brought upon herself an event which was seemingly another loss, but the sum of money the insurance company paid her allowed her to make the desired change in her life.

When we see the "why" behind the seeming accident, the state of consciousness that produced the accident, we are led to the conclusion that there is no accident. Everything in life has its in-visible meaning.

The man who learns of an accident, the man who knows "how" it happened, and the man who knows "why" it happened are on three different levels of awareness in regard to that accident. On the ascending scale, each higher level carries us a step in advance towards the truth of the accident.

We should strive constantly to lift ourselves to the higher level of meaning, the meaning that is always invisible and above the physical event. But, remember, the meaning or cause of the phenomena of life can be found only within the consciousness of man.

Man is so engrossed in the visible side of the drama of life - the side of "what" has happened, and "how" it happened - that he rarely rises to the invisible side of "why" it happened. He refuses to accept the Prophet's warning that:

> *Things which are seen were not made of things that do appear.*
>
> —Hebrews 11:3

His descriptions of "what" has happened and "how" it happened are true in terms of his corresponding level of thought, but when he asks "why" it happened, all physical explanations break down and he is forced to seek the "why", or meaning of it, on the invisible and higher level. The mechanical analysis of events deals only with external relationships of things. Such a course will never reach the level which holds the secret of why the events happen. Man must recognize that the lower and visible sides flow from the invisible and higher level of meaning.

Intuition is needed to lift us up to the level of meaning - to the level of why things happen. Let us follow the advice of the Hebrew prophet of old and "lift up our eyes unto the hills" within ourselves, and observe what is taking place there. See what ideas we have accepted as true, what states we have consented to, what dreams, what desires - and, above all, what intentions. It is from these hills that all things come to reveal our stature - our height - on the vertical scale of meaning. If we lift our eyes to "the Thee in Me who works behind the Veil", we will see the meaning of the phenomena of life.

Events appear on the screen of space to express the different levels of consciousness of man. A change in the level of his consciousness automatically results in a change of the phenomena of his life. To attempt to change conditions before he changes the level of consciousness from whence they came, is to struggle in vain. Man redeems the world as he ascends the vertical scale of meaning.

We saw, in the analogy of the book, that as consciousness was lifted up to the level where man could see meaning expressed in the arrangement of its letters, it also included the knowledge that the letters were arranged according to certain rules, and that such arrangements, when printed on paper and bound together, formed a book. What is true of the book is true of every event in the world.

> *They shall not hurt or destroy in all my holy mountain: for the earth shall be full of the knowledge of the Lord, as the waters cover the sea.*
>
> —Isaiah 11:9

Nothing is to be discarded; all is to be redeemed. Our lives, ascending the vertical scale of meaning towards an ever increasing awareness - an awareness of things of higher significance - are the process whereby this redemption is brought to pass.

As man arranges letters into words, and words into sentences to express meaning, in like manner, life arranges circumstances, conditions and events to express the unseen meanings or attitudes of men. Nothing is without significance. But man, not knowing the higher level of inner meaning, looks out upon a moving panorama of events and sees no meaning to life. There is always a level of meaning determining events and their essential relationship to our lives.

Here is a story that will enable us to seize the good in things seeming evil; to withhold judgment, and to act aright amid unsolved problems.

Just a few years ago, our country was shocked by a seeming injustice in our midst. The story was told on radio and television, as well as in the newspapers. You may recall the incident. The body of a young American soldier killed in Korea was returned to his home for burial. Just before the service, his wife was asked a routine question: Was her husband a Caucasian? When she replied that he was an Indian, burial was refused. This refusal was in accordance with the laws of that community, but it aroused the entire nation. We felt incensed that anyone who had been killed in the service of his country should be denied burial anywhere in his country. The story reached the attention of the President of the United States, and he offered burial with full military honors in Arlington National Cemetery. After the service, the wife told reporters that her husband had always dreamed of dying a hero, and having a hero's burial service with full military honors.

When, we in America, had to explain why progressive, intelligent people like ourselves, not only enacted but supported such laws in our great land of the free and the brave, we were hard put for an explanation. We, as observers, had seen only "what" happened, and "how" it happened. We failed to see "why" it happened.

That burial had to be refused if that lad was to realize his dream. We tried to explain the drama in terms of the lower level of "how" it happened, which explanation could not satisfy the one who had asked "why" it happened.

The true answer, viewed from the level of higher meaning, would be such a reversal of our common habits of thinking that it would be instantly rejected. The truth is that future states are causative of present facts - the Indian boy dreaming of a hero's death, with full military honors, was like Lady Macbeth transported "beyond this ignorant present", and could "feel now the future in the instant."

. . . and by it he being dead yet speaketh.

—Hebrews 11:4

CHAPTER 5

The Game of Life

I can easier teach twenty what were good to be done, than be one of the twenty to follow mine own teaching.

—Shakespeare

With this confession off my mind, I will now teach you how to play the game of life. Life is a game and, like all games, it has its aims and its rules.

In the little games that men concoct, such as cricket, tennis, baseball, football, and so on, the rules may be changed from time to time. After the changes are agreed upon, man must learn the new rules and play the game within the framework of the accepted rules.

However, in the game of life, the rules cannot be changed or broken. Only within the framework of its universal and everlastingly fixed rules can the game of life be played.

The game of life is played on the playing field of the mind.

In playing a game, the first thing we ask is: "What is its aim and purpose?" and the second, "What are the rules governing the game?" In the game of life, our chief aim is towards increasing awareness - an awareness of things of greater significance; and our second aim is towards achieving our goals, realizing our desires.

As to our desires, the rules reach only so far as to indicate the way in which we should go to realize them, but the desires themselves must be the individual's own concern. The rules governing the game of life are simple, but it takes a lifetime of practice to use them wisely. Here is one of the rules:

As he thinketh in his heart, so is he.

—Proverbs 23:7

Thinking is usually believed to be a function entirely untrammeled and free, without any rules to constrain it. But that is not true. Thinking moves by its own processes in a bounded territory, with definite paths and patterns. Thinking follows the tracks laid down in one's own inner conversations.

All of us can realize our objectives by the wise use of mind and speech.

Most of us are totally unaware of the mental activity which goes on within us. But to play the game of life successfully, we must become aware of our every mental activity, for this activity, in the form of inner conversations, is the cause of the outer phenomena of our life.

> *. . . every idle word that man shall speak, they shall give account thereof in the day of judgment.*
>
> *For by thy words thou shall be justified, and by thy words thou shalt be condemned.*
>
> —Matthew 12:36, 37

The law of the Word cannot be broken.

> *. . .A bone of him shall not be broken.*
>
> —John 19:36

The law of the Word never overlooks an inner word nor makes the smallest allowance for our ignorance of its power. It fashions life about us as we, by our inner conversations, fashion life within ourselves. This is done to reveal to us our position on the playing field of life. There is no opponent in the game of life; there is only the goal.

Not long ago, I was discussing this with a successful and philanthropic business man. He told me a thought provoking story about himself.

He said, "You know, Neville, I first learned about goals in life when I was fourteen, and it was on the playing field at school. I was good at track and had a fine day, but there was one more race to run, and I had stiff competition in one other boy. I was determined to beat him. I beat him, it is true; but while I was keeping my eye on him, a third boy, who was considered no competition at all, won the race."

"That experience taught me a lesson I have used throughout my life. When people ask me about my success, I must say, that I believe it is because I have never made 'making money' my goal. My goal is the wise, productive use of money."

This man's inner conversations are based on the premise that he already has money; his constant inner question: the proper use of it.

The inner conversations of the man struggling to 'get' money only prove his lack of money.

In his ignorance of the power of the word, he is building barriers in the way of the attainment of his goal; he has his eye on the competition rather than on the goal itself.

> *The fault, dear Brutus, is not in our stars, But in ourselves, that we are underlings.*
>
> —Julius Caesar: Act I, Scene II

As "the worlds were framed by the Word of God," so we as "imitators of God as dear children" create the conditions and circumstances of our lives by our all-powerful human inner words.

Without practice, the most profound knowledge of the game would produce no desired results.

"To him that knoweth to do good" — that is, knoweth the rules — "and doeth it not, to him it is sin". In other words, he will miss his mark and fail to realize his goal.

In the parable of the Talents, the Master's condemnation of the servant who neglected to use his gift is clear and unmistakable, and having discovered one of the rules of the game of life, we risk failure by ignoring it. The talent not used, like the limb not exercised, slumbers and finally atrophies. We must be "doers of the Word, and not hearers only". Since thinking follows the tracks laid down in one's own inner conversations, not only can we see where we are going on the playing field of life by observing our inner conversations, but also, we can determine where we will go by controlling and directing our inner talking.

What would you think and say and do were you already the one you want to be? Begin to think and say and do this inwardly. You are told that "there is a rod in heaven that revealeth secrets," and, you must always remember that heaven is within you; and to make it crystal clear who God is, where He is, and what His secrets are, Daniel continues, "Thy dream, and the visions of thy head are these". They reveal the tracks to which you are tied, and point the direction in which you are going.

This is what one woman did to turn the tracks to which she had been unhappily tied in the direction in which she wanted to go. For two years, she had kept herself estranged from the three people she loved most. She had had a quarrel with her daughter-in-law, who ordered her from her home. For those two years, she had not seen or heard from her son, her daughter-in-law or her grandson, though she had sent her grandson numerous gifts in the meantime. Every time she thought of her family, which was daily, she carried on a mental conversation with her daughter-in-law, blaming her for the quarrel and accusing her of being selfish.

Upon hearing a lecture of mine one night - it was this very lecture on the game of life and how to play it - she suddenly realized she was the cause of the prolonged silence and that she, and she alone, must do something about it. Recognizing that her goal was to have the former loving relationship, she set herself the task of completely changing her inner talking.

That very night, in her imagination, she constructed two loving, tender letters written to her, one from her daughter-in-law and the other from her grandson. In her imagination, she read them over and over again until she fell asleep in the joyful mood of having received the letters. She repeated this imaginary act each night for eight nights. On the morning of the ninth day, she received one envelope containing two letters, one from her daughter-in-law, one from her grandson. They were loving, tender letters inviting her to visit them, almost replicas of those she had constructed mentally. By using her imagination consciously and lovingly, she had turned the tracks to which she was tied, in the direction she wanted to go, towards a happy family reunion.

A change of attitude is a change of position on the playing field of life. The game of life is not being played out there in what is called space and time; the real moves in the game of life take place within, on the playing field of the mind.

Losing thy soul, thy soul
Again to find;
Rendering toward that goal
Thy separate mind.

—Laurence Housman

CHAPTER 6

Time, Times, and a Half

> *And one said to the man clothed in linen, which was upon the waters of the river, 'How long shall it be to the end of these wonders?' And I heard the man clothed in linen, which was upon the waters of the river, when he held up his right hand and his left hand unto heaven, and swear by him that 'liveth forever that it shall be for a time, times, and an half.'*
>
> —Daniel 12:6, 7

At one of my lectures given in Los Angeles on the subject of the hidden meaning behind the stories of the Bible, someone asked me to interpret the above quotation from the Book of Daniel. After I confessed I did not know the meaning of that particular passage, a lady in the audience said to herself, "If the mind behaves according to the assumption with which it starts, then I will find the true answer to that question and tell it to Neville." And this is what she told me.

"Last night the question was asked: 'What is the meaning of "time, times, and an half" as recorded in Daniel 12:7?' Before going to sleep last night I said to myself, 'Now there is a simple answer to this question, so I will assume that I know it. And while I am sleeping, my greater self will find the answer and reveal it to my lesser self in dream or vision.'"

"Around five a.m., I awakened. It was too early to rise, so remaining in bed I quickly fell into that half dreamy state between waking and sleeping, and while in that state a picture came into my mind of an old lady. She was sitting in a rocking chair and rocking back and forth, back and forth. Then a voice which sounded like your voice said to me: 'Do it over and over and over again until it takes on the tones of reality.'"

"I jumped out of bed and re-read the Twelfth Chapter of Daniel, and this is the intuitive answer I received. Taking the sixth and seventh verses, for they constituted last night's question, I felt that if the garments with which Biblical characters are clothed correspond to their level of consciousness, as you teach, then linen must represent a very high level of consciousness indeed; for the 'man clothed in linen' was standing 'upon the waters of the river', and if, as you teach, water symbolizes a high level of psychological truth, then the individual who could walk upon it must truly represent an exalted state of consciousness. I therefore felt that what he had to say must indeed be very significant. Now the question asked of him was 'How long shall it be to the end of these wonders?' And his answer was, 'A time, times, and an half.' Remembering my vision of the old lady rocking back and forth, and your voice telling me to 'do it over and over and over again until it takes on the tones of reality', and remembering that this vision and your instruction came to me in response to my assumption that I knew the answer, I intuitively felt that the question asked the 'man clothed in linen' meant how long shall it be until the wonderful dreams that I am dreaming become a reality. And his answer is, 'Do it over and over and over again until it takes on the tones of reality'. 'A time' means to perform the imaginary action which implies the fulfillment of the wish. 'Times' mean to repeat the imaginary action over and over again, and 'an half' means the moment of falling asleep while performing the imaginary action, for such a moment usually arrives before the pre-determined action is completed and, therefore, can be said to be a half or part of a time."

To get such inner understanding of the Scriptures by the simple assumption that she did know the answer, was a wonderful experience for this woman. However, to know the true meaning of "time, times, and an half" she must apply her understanding in her daily life. We are never at a loss in an opportunity to test this understanding, either for ourselves or for another.

A number of years ago, a widow living in the same apartment house as we, came to see me about her cat. The cat was her constant companion and dear to her heart. He was, however, eight years old, very ill and in great pain. He had not eaten for days and would not move from under her bed. Two veterinarians had seen the cat and advised the woman that the cat could not be cured, and that he should be put to sleep immediately. I suggested that that night, before retiring, she create in her imagination some action that would indicate the cat was its former healthy self. I advised her to do it over and over again until it took on the tones of reality.

This, she promised to do. However, either from lack of faith in my advice or from lack of faith in her own ability to carry out the imaginary action, she asked her niece to spend the night with her.

This request was made so that if the cat were not well by morning, the niece could take it to the veterinarian's and she, the owner, would not have to face such a dreaded task herself. That night, she settled herself in an easy chair and began to imagine the cat was romping beside her, scratching at the furniture and doing many things she would not normally have allowed. Each time she found that her mind had wandered from its pre-determined task to see a normal, healthy, frisky cat, she brought her attention back to the room and started her imaginary action over again. This she did over and over again until, finally, in a feeling of relief, she dropped off to sleep, still seated in her chair.

At about four o'clock in the morning, she was awakened by the cry of her cat. He was standing by her chair. After attracting her attention, he led her to the kitchen where he begged for food. She fixed him a little warm milk which he quickly drank, and cried for more.

That cat lived comfortably for five more years, when, without pain or illness, he died naturally in his sleep.

> *How long shall it be to the end of these wonders? A time, times, and an half. In a dream in a vision of the night, when deep sleep falleth upon men, in slumberings upon the bed; Then he openeth the ears of men, and sealeth their instructions.*
>
> —Job 33:15, 16

CHAPTER 7

Be Ye Wise as Serpents

. . .be ye therefore wise as serpents, and harmless as doves.

—Matthew 10:16

The serpent's ability to form its skin by ossifying a portion of itself, and its skill in shedding each skin as it outgrew it, caused man to regard this reptile as a symbol of the power of endless growth and self-reproduction. Man is told, therefore, to be "wise as the serpent" and learn how to shed his skin - his environment - which is his solidified self; man must learn how to "loose him, and let him go" . . . how to "put off the old man" . . .how to die to the old and yet know, like the serpent, that he "shall not surely die".

Man has not learned as yet that all that is outside his physical body is also a part of himself, that his world and all the conditions of his life are but the outpicturing of his state of consciousness.

When he knows this truth, he will stop the futile struggle of self-contention and, like the serpent, let the old go and grow a new environment.

> *Man is immortal; therefore he must die endlessly. For life is a creative idea; it can only find itself in changing forms.*
>
> —Rabindranath Tagore

In ancient times, serpents were also associated with the guardianship of treasure or wealth. The injunction to be "wise as serpents" is the advice to man to awaken the power of his subtilized body - his imagination - that he, like the serpent, may grow and outgrow, die and yet not die, for from such deaths and resurrections alone, shedding the old and putting on the new, shall come fulfillment of his dreams and the finding of his treaures. As "the serpent was more subtile than any beast of the field which the Lord God had made" - Genesis 3:1 - even so, imagination is more subtile than any creature of the heavens which the Lord God had created. Imagination is the creature that:

> *. . .was made subject to vanity, not willingly, but by reason of him who hath subjected the same in hope...*

> *For we are saved by hope : but hope that is seen is not hope: for what a man seeth, why doth he yet hope for it?*
>
> *But if we hope for that we see not, then do we have patience wait for it.*
>
> —Romans 8:20; 24, 25

Although the outer, or "natural", man of the senses is interlocked with his environment, the inner, or spiritual, man of imagination is not thus interlocked. If the interlocking were complete, the charge to be "wise as serpents" would be in vain. Were we completely interlocked with our environment, we could not withdraw our attention from the evidence of the senses and feel ourselves into the situation of our fulfilled desire, in hope that that unseen state would solidify as our new environment. But:

> *There is a natural body, and there is a spiritual body.*
>
> —1 Corinthians 15:44

The spiritual body of imagination is not interlocked with man's environment. The spiritual body can withdraw from the outer man of sense and environment and imagine itself to be what it wants to be. And if it remains faithful to the vision, imagination will build for man a new environment in which to live. This is what is meant by the statement:

> *. . .I go to prepare a place for you. And if I go and prepare a place for you, I will come again, and receive you unto myself; that where I am, there ye may be also.*
>
> —John 14:2, 3

The place that is prepared for you need not be a place in space. It can be health, wealth, companionship, anything that you desire in this world. Now, how is the place prepared?

You must first construct as life-like a representation as possible of what you would see and hear and do if you were physically present and physically moving about in that "place." Then, with your physical body immobilized, you must imagine that you are actually in that "place" and are seeing and hearing and doing all that you would see and hear and do if you were there physically. This you must do over and over again until it takes on the tones of reality. When it feels natural, the "place" has been prepared as the new environment for your outer or physical self. Now you may open your physical eyes and return to your former state. The "place" is prepared, and where you have been in imagination, there you shall be in the body also.

How this imagined state is realized physically is not the concern of you, the natural or outer man.

The spiritual body, on its return from the imagined state to its former physical state, created an invisible bridge of incident to link the two states. Although the curious feeling that you were actually there and that the state was real is gone, as soon as you open your eyes upon the old familiar environment, nevertheless, you are haunted with the sense of a double identity - with the knowledge that "there is a natural body, and there is a spiritual body." When you, the natural man, have had this experience you will go automatically across the bridge of events which leads to the physical realization of your invisibly prepared place.

This concept - that man is dual and that the inner man of imagination can dwell in future states and return to the present moment with a bridge of events to link the two - clashes violently with the widely accepted view about the human personality and the cause and nature of phenomena. Such a concept demands a revolution in current ideas about the human personality, and about space, time and matter. The concept that man, consciously or unconsciously, determines the conditions of life by imagining himself into these mental states, leads to the conclusion that this supposedly solid world is a construction of Mind - a concept which, at first, common sense rejects. However, we should remember that most of the concepts which common sense at first rejected, man was afterward forced to accept. These never-ending reversals of judgment which experience has forced upon man led Professor Whitehead to write:

> *Heaven knows what seeming nonsense may not tomorrow be demonstrated truth.*

The creative power in man sleeps and needs to be awakened.

> *Awake thou that sleepest, and arise from the dead.*
>
> —Ephesians 5:14

Wake from the sleep that tells you the outer world is the cause of the conditions of your life. Rise from the dead past and create a new environment.

> *Know ye not that ye are the temple of God, and that the Spirit of God dwelleth in you?*
>
> —1 Corinthians 3:16

The Spirit of God in you is your imagination, but it sleeps and needs to be awakened, in order to lift you off the bar of the senses where you have so long lain stranded.

The boundless possibilities open to you as you become "wise as serpents" is beyond measure.

You will select the ideal conditions you want to experience and the ideal environment you want to live in. Experiencing these states in imagination until they have sensory vividness, you will externalize them as surely as the serpent now externalizes its skin.

After you have outgrown them, then, you will cast them off as easily as "the snake throws her enamell'd skin". The more abundant life - the whole purpose of Creation - cannot be saved through death and resurrection.

God desired form, so He became man: and it is not enough for us to recognize His spirit at work in creation, we must see His work in form and say that it is good, even though we outgrow the form, forever and ever.

He leads
Through widening chambers of delight to where
Throbs rapture near an end that aye recedes,
Because His touch is Infinite and lends
A yonder to all ends.

And, I, if I be lifted up from the earth, will draw all men unto me.

—John 12:32

If I be lifted up from the evidence of the senses to the state of consciousness I desire to realize and remain in that state until it feels natural. I will form that state around me and all men will see it.

But how to persuade man this is true - that imaginative life is the only living; that assuming the feeling of the wish fulfilled is the way to the more abundant life and not the compensation of the escapist - that is the problem.

To see as "though widening chambers of delight" what living in the realms of imagination means, to appreciate and enjoy the world, one must live imaginatively; one must dream and occupy his dream, then grow and outgrow the dream, forever and ever.

The unimaginative man, who will not lose his life on one level that he may find it on a higher level, is nothing but a Lot's wife - a pillar of self-satisfied salt. On the other hand, those who refuse form as being unspiritual and who reject incarnation as separate from God are ignorant of the great mystery: "Great is the mystery, God was manifest in the flesh."

Your life expresses one thing, and one thing only, your state of consciousness. Everything is dependent upon that.

As you, through the medium of imagination, assume a state of consciousness, that state begins to clothe itself in form, It solidifies around you as the serpent's skin ossifies around it. But you must be faithful to the state. You must not go from state to state, but, rather, wait patiently in the one invisible state until it takes on form and becomes an objective fact.

Patience is necessary, but patience will be easy after your first success in shedding the old and growing the new, for we are able to wait according as we have been rewarded by understanding in the past.

Understanding is the secret of patience.

What natural joy and spontaneous delight lie in seeing the world - not with, but as Blake says - through the eye! Imagine that you are seeing what you want to see, and remain faithful to your vision. Your imagination will make for itself a corresponding form in which to live.

All things are made by imagination's power. Nothing begins except in the imagination of man.

"From within out" is the law of the universe.

"As within, so without." Man turns outward in his search for truth, but the essential thing is to look within.

Truth is within ourselves; it takes no rise
From outward things, whate'er you may believe.
There is an inmost center in us all,
Where truth abides in fullness .. . and to know,
Rather consist in opening out a way
Whence the imprisoned splendor may escape,
Than in effecting entry for a light
Supposed to be without.

—Browning: "Paracelsus"

I think you will be interested in an instance of how a young woman shed the skin of resentment and put on a far different kind of skin. The parents of this woman had separated when she was six years old and she had lived with her mother. She rarely saw her father. But once a year he sent her a five dollar check for Christmas. Following her marriage, he did increase the Christmas gift to ten dollars.

After one of my lectures, she was dwelling on my statement that man's suspicion of another is only a measure of his own deceitfulness, and she recognized that she had been harboring resentment towards her father for years. That night she resolved to let go her resentment and put a fond reaction in its place. In her imagination, she felt she was embracing her father in the warmest way. She did it over and over again until she caught the spirit of her imaginary act, and then she fell asleep in a very contented mood.

The following day she happened to pass through the fur department of one of our large stores in California. For some time she had been toying with the idea of having a new fur scarf, but felt she could not afford it. This time her eye was caught by a stone marten scarf, and she picked it up and tried it on. After feeling it and seeing herself in it, reluctantly she took off the scarf and returned it to the salesman, telling herself she really could not afford it. As she was leaving the department, she stopped and thought, "Neville tells we can have whatever we desire if we will only capture the feeling of already having it." In her imagination, she put the scarf back on, felt the reality of it, and went about her shopping, all the while enjoying the imagined wearing of it.

This young woman never associated these two imaginary acts. In fact, she had almost forgotten what she had done until, a few weeks later, on Mother's Day, the doorbell rang unexpectedly.

There was her father. As she embraced him, she remembered her first imaginary action. As she opened the package he had brought her - the first gift in these many years - she remembered her second imaginary action, for the box contained a beautiful stone marten scarf.

> *Ye are gods; and all of you are children of the most High.*
>
> —Psalms 82:6

> *"...be ye therefore wise as serpents, and harmless as doves.*
>
> —Matthew 10:16

CHAPTER 8

The Water and the Blood

...Except a man be born again he cannot see the kingdom of God.

—John 3:3

"But one of the soldiers with a spear pierced his side, and forthwith came there out blood and water.

—John 19:34

"This is he that came by water and blood, even Jesus Christ; not by water only, but by water and blood.

—1 John 5:6

According to the gospel and the Epistle of John, not only must man be "born again" but he must be born again of water and blood. These two inward experiences are linked with two outward rites –

baptism and communion. But the two outward rites – baptism to symbolize birth by water, and the wine of communion to symbolize acceptance of the blood of the Savoir, cannot produce the real birth or radical transformation of the individual, which is promised to man. The outward use of water and wine cannot bring about the desired change of mind. We must, therefore, look for the hidden meaning behind the symbols of water and blood.

The Bible uses many images to symbolize Truth, but the images used symbolize Truth on different levels of meaning. On the lowest level, the image used is stone. For example:

> *… a great stone was upon the well's mouth. And thither were all the flocks gathered: and they rolled the stone from the well's mouth, and watered the sheep…*
>
> —Genesis 29:2, 3

> *"…They sank into the bottom as a stone.*
>
> —Exodus 15:5

When a stone blocks the well, it means that people have taken these great symbolical revelations of truth literally. When someone rolls the stone away, it means that an individual has discovered beneath the allegory or parable its psychological life germ, or meaning. This hidden meaning which lies behind the literal words is symbolized by water. It is this water. In the form of psychological Truth, that he then offers to humanity.

> *The flock of my pasture are men.*
>
> —Ezekiel 34:31

The literal-minded man who refuses the "cup of water" – psychological Truth – offered him, "sinks into the bottom as a stone." He remains on the level where he sees everything in pure objectivity, without any subjective relationship he may keep all the commandments – written on stone – literally, and yet break them psychologically all day long.

He may, for example not literally steal the property of another, and yet see the other in want. To see another in want, is to rob him of his birthright as a child of God. For we are all "children of the most high."

> *And if children, then heirs; heirs of God, and joint-heirs with Christ...*
>
> —Romans 8:17

To know what to do about a seeming misfortune is to have the "cup of water" – the psychological Truth – that could save the situation. But such knowledge is not enough. Man must not only "fill the water pots of stone with water" – that is, discover the psychological truth – into wine.

This he does by living a life according to the truth which he has discovered.

Only by such use of the truth can he "taste the water that was made wine" [John 2:9].

A mans birthright is to be Jesus. He is born to "save his people from their sins" [Matthew 1 : 21].

But the salvation of a man is "not by water only, but by water and blood."

To know what to do to save yourself or another is not enough; you must do it. Knowledge of what to do is water; doing it is blood.

This is he that came not by water only, but by water and blood." The whole of this mystery is in the conscious, active use of imagination to appropriate that particular state of consciousness that would save you or another from the present limitation. Outward ceremonies cannot accomplish this.

> *... there shall meet you a man bearing a pitcher of water; follow him. And wheresoever he shall go in, say ye to the goodman of the house, The Master saith, Where is the guest-chamber, where I shall eat the Passover with my disciples? And he will show you a large upper room furnished and prepared: there make ready for us.*
>
> —Luke 22:10-12

Whatever you desire is already "furnished and prepared".

Your imagination can put you in touch inwardly with that state of consciousness. If you imagine that you are already the one you want to be, you are following the "man bearing a pitcher of water". If you remain in that state, you have entered the guest-chamber – Passover – and committed your spirit into the hands of God – your consciousness.

A man's state of consciousness is his demand on the Infinite Store House of God, and, like the law of commerce, a demand creates a supply.

To change the supply, you change the demand – your state of consciousness.

What you desire to be, that you must feel you already are. Your state of consciousness creates the conditions of your life, rather than the conditions create your state of consciousness. To know this Truth, is to have the "water of life".

But your savior – the solution of your problem – cannot be manifested by such knowledge only.

It can be realized only as such knowledge is applied.

Only as you assume the feeling of your wish fulfilled, and continue therein, is your side pierced; from whence cometh blood and water". In this manner only is Jesus – the solution of your problem – realized.

> *...for thou must know that in the government of the mind, thou art thine own lord and master, that there will rise up no fire in the circle or whole circumference of thy body and spirit, unless thou awakes it thyself.*

God is your consciousness.

His promises are conditional. Unless the demand – your state of consciousness – is changed, the supply – the present conditions of your life remain as they are. "As we forgive" – as we change our mind – the law is automatic.

Your state of consciousness is the spring of action, the directing force, and that which creates the supply.

> *...if that nation, against whom I have pronounced, turn from their evil, I will repent of the evil that I thought to do unto them. And at what instant I shall speak concerning a nation, and concerning a kingdom, to build and to plant it; If it do evil in my sight, that it obey not my voice, then I will repent of the good, wherewith I said I would benefit them.*
>
> —Jeremiah 18:8, 9, 10

This statement of Jeremiah suggests that a commitment is involved if the individual or nation would realize the goal – a commitment to certain fixed attitudes of mind. The feeling of the wish fulfilled is a necessary condition in mans search for the goal.

The story I am about to tell you shows that man is what the observer has the capacity to see in him; that what he is seen to be is a direct index to the observer's state of consciousness.

This story is, also, a challenge to us all to shed our blood" – use our imagination lovingly on behalf of another.

There is no day that passes that does not afford us the opportunity to transform a life by the shedding of our blood".

> *Without the shedding of blood there is no remission.*
>
> —Hebrews 9:22

One night in New York City, I was able to unveil the mystery of the "water and the blood" to a school teacher. I had quoted the above statement from Hebrews 9:22 and went on to explain that the realization that we have no hope save in ourselves is the discovery that God is within us; that this discovery causes the dark caverns of the skull to grow luminous. And we know that: "The spirit of man is the candle of the lord" [Proverbs 20:27]; and that this realization is the light to guide us safely over the earth.

His Candle shined upon my head and by his light I walked through darkness.

—Job 29:3

However, we must not look upon this radiant light of the head as God, for man is the image of God.

God appears, and God is light,
To those poor souls who dwell in Night;
But does a Human Form display
To those who dwell in realms of Day.

—Blake

But this must be experienced to be known. There is no other way, and no other man's experience can be a substitute for our own.

I told the teacher that her change of attitude in regard to another would produce a corresponding change in the other; that such knowledge was the true meaning of the water mentioned in 1 John 5:6, but that such knowledge alone was not enough to produce the re-birth desired; that such re-birth could only come to pass by "water and blood", or the application of this truth.

Knowledge of what to do is the water of life, but doing it is the blood of the savior.

In other words, a little knowledge, if carried out in action is more profitable than much knowledge which we neglect to carry out in action.

As I talked, one student kept impinging upon the teachers mind. But this, thought she, would be a too difficult case on which to test the truth of what I was telling her concerning the mystery of re-birth. All knew, teachers and students alike, that this particular student was incorrigible.

The outer facts of her case were these: The teachers, including the principal and school psychiatrist, had sat in judgment on the student just a few days before. They had come to a unanimous decision that the girl, for the good of the school, must be expelled upon reaching her sixteenth birthday. She was rude, crude, unethical and used most vile language. The date for dismissal was but a month away.

As she rode home that night, the teacher kept wondering if she could really change her mind about the girls, and if so, would the student undergo a change of behavior because she herself had undergone a change of attitude?

The only way to find out would be to try. This would be quite an undertaking for it meant assuming full responsibility for the incarnation of the new values in the student. Did she dare to assume so great a power – such creative, God-like power? This meant a complete reversal of man's normal attitude towards life from "I will love him if he first loves me", to "He loves me, because I first loved him." This was too much like playing God.

We love him, because he first loved us.

—1 John 4:19

But no matter how she tried to argue against it, the feeling persisted that my interpretation gave meaning to the mystery of re-birth by "water and blood." The teacher decided to accept the challenge. And this is what she did.

She brought the child's face before her mind's eye and saw her smile. She listened and imagined she heard the girl say "Good morning". This was something the student had never done since coming to that school. The teacher imagined the very best about the girl, and then listened and looked as though she heard and saw all that she would hear and see after these things should be. The teacher did this over and over again until she persuaded herself it was true, and fell asleep.

The very next morning, the student entered her classroom and smilingly said "Good morning". The teacher was so surprised she almost did not respond, and, by her own confession, all through the day she looked for signs of the girl's returning to her former behavior. However, the girl continued in the transformed state. By the end of the week, the change was noted by all; a second staff meeting was called and a decision of expulsion was revoked. As the child remained friendly and gracious, the teacher has had to ask herself, "Where was the bad child in the first place?"

For Mercy, Pity, Peace, and Love Is God,
Our father dear,
And Mercy, Pity, Peace, and Love Is man,
His child and care."

—Blake, *The Divine Image*

Transformation is in principle always possible, for the transformed being lives in us, and it is only a question of becoming conscious of it.

The teacher had to experience this transformation to know the mystery of "blood and water"; there was no other way, and no mans experience could have been a substitute for her own.

We have redemption through his blood.

—Ephesians 1:7

Without the decision to change her mind in regard to the child, and the imaginative power to carry it out, the teacher could never have redeemed the student. None can know the redemptive power of the imagination who has not "shed his blood", and tasted the cup of experience.

Once read thy own breast right,
And thou hast done with fears!
Man gets no other light,
Search he a thousand years.

—Matthew Arnold

CHAPTER 9

A Mystical View

And with many such parables spake he the word unto them, as they were able to hear it. But without a parable spake he not unto them: and when they were alone, he expounded all things to his disciples.

—Mark 4:33, 34

This collection of parables which is called the bible is a revelation of Truth expressed in symbolism to reveal the Laws and purposes of the mind of man. As we become aware of deeper meanings in the parables than those which are usually assigned to them, we are apprehending them mystically.

For example, let us take a mystical view of the advice given to the disciples in Matthew 10:10. We read that as the disciples were ready to teach and practice the great laws of mind which had been revealed to them, they were told not to provide shoes for the journey. A disciple is one who disciplines his mind that he may consciously function and act on higher and higher levels of consciousness. The shoe was chosen as a symbol of vicarious atonement or the spirit of "let-me-do-it-for-you", because the shoe protects the wearer and shields him from impurities by taking them upon himself. The aim of the disciple is always to lead himself and others from the bondage of dependency into the liberty of the Sons of God. Hence the advice, take no shoes. Accept no intermediary between yourself and God. Turn from all who would offer to do for you what you should do, and could, do far better yourself.

> *Earth's crammed with Heaven,*
> *And every common bush afire with God,*
> *But only he who sees takes off his shoes.*
>
> —Elizabeth Barrett Browning

> *"Verily I say unto you, inasmuch as ye have done it unto one of the least of these my breathren, Ye have done it unto me.*
>
> —Matthew 25:40

Every time you exercise your imagination on behalf of another, be it good, bad or indifferent, you have literally done that to Christ, for Christ is awakened Human Imagination. Through the wise and loving use of imagination, man clothes and feeds

Christ, and through ignorant and fearful misuse of imagination, man disrobes and scourges Christ.

"Let none of you imagine evil in your hearts against your neighbor" [Zechariah 8:17] is sound but negative advice. A man may stop misusing his imagination on the advice of a friend; he may be negatively served by the experience of others and learn not to imagine, but that is not enough. Such lack of use of the creative power of imagination could never clothe and feed Christ. The purple robe of the Son of God is woven, not by not imagining evil, but by imaging the good; by the active, voluntary and loving use of imagination.

> *Whatsoever things are of good report; if there be any virtue, and if there be any praise, think on these things.*
>
> —Philippians 4:8

> *"King Solomon made himself a chariot of the wood of Lebanon. He made the pillars thereof of silver, the bottom thereof of gold, the covering of it of purple, the midst thereof being paved with love…*
>
> —Song of Solomon 3: 9, 10

The first thing we notice is "King Solomon made himself". That is what every man must eventually do – make himself a chariot of the wood of Lebanon. By chariot, the writer of this allegory means Mind, in which stands the spirit of Wisdom – Solomon – controlling the four functions of Mind that he may build a world of Love and Truth.

"And Joseph made ready his chariot and went up to meet Israel his father." "What tributaries follow him to Rome to grace in captive bonds his chariot wheels?" If man does not make himself a chariot of the wood of Lebanon, then his will be like Queen Mab's: "She is the fairies' midwife; … her chariot is an empty hazelnut."

The wood of Lebanon was the mystic's symbol of incorruptibility. To a mystic, It is obvious what King Solomon made himself. Silver typified knowledge, gold symbolized wisdom, and purple – clothed or covered the incorruptible Mind with the red of Love and the blue of Truth.

And they clothed him with purple.

—Mark 15:17

Incarnate, incorruptible four-fold wisdom, clothed in purple. Love and Truth – the purpose of man's experience on earth.

Love is the sage's stone;
It takes gold from the clod;
It turns naught into aught,
Transforms me into God.

—Angelus Silesius